Domestic Violence

ALSO BY EAVAN BOLAND

New Territory

The War Horse

Night Feed

The Journey

Selected Poems: 1989

Outside History: Selected Poems, 1980–1990

In a Time of Violence

An Origin Like Water: Collected Poems, 1967–1987

The Lost Land

Object Lessons: The Life of the Woman and the Poet in Our Time

The Making of a Poem (edited with Mark Strand)

Against Love Poetry

DOMESTIC
VIOLENCE

POEMS

Eavan Boland

W. W. NORTON & COMPANY
New York • London

Copyright © 2007 by Eavan Boland

All rights reserved
Printed in the United States of America
First Edition

For information about permission to reproduce selections from
this book, write to Permissions, W. W. Norton & Company, Inc.,
500 Fifth Avenue, New York, NY 10110

Manufacturing by Courier Westford
Book design by Charlotte Staub
Production manager: Julia Druskin

Library of Congress Cataloging-in-Publication Data
Boland, Eavan.
    Domestic violence : poems / Eavan Boland. — 1st ed.
        p. cm.
Includes bibliographical references and index.
    ISBN-13: 978-0-393-06241-0 (hardcover)
    ISBN-10: 0-393-06241-4 (hardcover)
    I. Title.
PR6052.035D66 2007
821' .914—dc22

                                        2006036389

W. W. Norton & Company, Inc., 500 Fifth Avenue,
New York, N.Y. 10110
www.wwnorton.com

W. W. Norton & Company Ltd., Castle House, 75/76 Wells Street,
London W1T 3QT

1 2 3 4 5 6 7 8 9 0

For
Frances Kelly
1908–2002

CONTENTS

Domestic Violence

1. Domestic Violence 13
2. How the Dance Came to the City 16
3. How It Was Once in Our Country 18
4. Still Life 19
5. Silenced 21
6. Histories 22
7. Wisdom 23
8. Irish Interior 25
9. In Our Own Country 27

Letters to the Dead

Amber 31
An Elegy for my Mother in Which She Scarcely Appears 33
And Soul 35
Secrets 37
On This Earth 38
Inheritance 39
Traveler 41
Windfall 42
Letters to the Dead 43

Indoors

To Memory 47

Of Shadow. Of Simile 49

Indoors 50

In Season 52

The Room in Which My First Child Slept 54

Midnight on the Sixth Day 55

Neighbors 56

Falling Asleep to the Sound of Rain 57

Becoming the Hand of John Speed

Atlantis—A Lost Sonnet 63

Becoming the Hand of John Speed 64

Papers 66

Formation 68

On Seeing James Malton's Powerscourt-House, Dublin 1795 70

The Nineteenth-Century Irish Poets 72

The Origins of Our Native Speech 73

Violence Against Women 75

Instructions 77

In Coming Days 78

ACKNOWLEDGMENTS

Acknowledgments are made to the editors of the following publications in which some of these poems appeared.

The New Yorker
The Atlantic Monthly
The New Republic
The Yale Review
The Paris Review
Threepenny Review
Shenandoah
P.N. Review
Poetry
The Kenyon Review
Tiimes Literary Supplement
The Nation
Poetry Review (UK)

My thanks to Jody Allen-Randolph, Jill Bialosky, Kevin Casey, and Michael Schmidt.

DOMESTIC VIOLENCE

1. *Domestic Violence*

1.

It was winter, lunar, wet. At dusk
Pewter seedlings became moonlight orphans.
Pleased to meet you meat to please you
said the butcher's sign in the window in the village.

Everything changed the year that we got married.
And after that we moved out to the suburbs.
How young we were, how ignorant, how ready
to think the only history was our own.

And there was a couple who quarreled into the night,
Their voices high, sharp:
nothing is ever entirely
right in the lives of those who love each other.

2.

In that season suddenly our island
Broke out its old sores for all to see.
We saw them too.
We stood there wondering how

the salt horizons and the Dublin hills,
the rivers, table mountains, Viking marshes
we thought we knew
had been made to shiver

into our ancient twelve by fifteen television
which gave them back as gray and grayer tears
and killings, killings, killings,
then moonlight-colored funerals:

nothing we said
not then, not later,
fathomed what it is
is wrong in the lives of those who hate each other.

3.

And if the provenance of memory is
only that—remember, not atone—
and if I can be safe in
the weak spring light in that kitchen, then

why is there another kitchen, spring light
always darkening in it and
a woman whispering to a man
over and over *what else could we have done?*

4.

We failed our moment or our moment failed us.
The times were grand in size and we were small.
Why do I write that
when I don't believe it?

We lived our lives, were happy, stayed as one.
Children were born and raised here
and are gone,
including ours.

As for that couple did we ever
find out who they were
and did we want to?
I think we know. I think we always knew.

2. How the Dance Came to the City

It came with the osprey, the cormorants, the air
at the edge of the storm, on the same route as
the blight and with the nightly sweats that said *fever*.

It came with the scarlet tunics and rowel spurs,
with the epaulettes and their poisonous drizzle of gold,
with the boots, the gloves, the whips, the flash of the cuirasses.

It came with a sail riding the empire-blue haze
of the horizon growing closer, gaining and then
it was there: the whole creaking orchestra of salt and canvas.

And here is the cargo, deep in the hold of the ship,
stored with the coiled ropes and crated spice and coal,
the lumber and boredom of arrival, underneath

timbers shifting and clicking from the turnaround
of the tides locked at the mouth of Dublin Bay, is
the two-step, the quick step, the whirl, the slow return.

Tonight in rooms where skirts appear steeped in tea
when they are only deep in shadow and where heat
collects at the waist, the wrist, is wet at the base of the neck,

the secrets of the dark will be the truths of the body
a young girl feels and hides even from herself as she lets fall
satin from her thighs to her ankles, as she lets herself think

how it started, just where: with the minuet, the quadrille,
the chandeliers glinting, the noise wild silk makes and
her face flushed and wide-eyed in the mirror of his sword.

3. How It Was Once in Our Country

In those years I owned a blue plate,
blue from the very edges to the center,
ocean-blue, the sort of under-wave blue
a mermaid could easily dive down into and enter.

When I looked at the plate I saw the mouth
of a harbor, an afternoon without a breath
of air, the evening clear all the way to Howth
and back, the sky a paler blue farther to the south.

Consider the kind of body that enters blueness,
made out of dead-end myth and mischievous
whispers of an old, borderless
existence where the body's meaning is both more and less.

Sea trawler, land siren: succubus to all the dreams
land has of ocean, of its old home.
She must have witnessed deaths. Of course she did.
Some say she stayed down there to escape the screams.

4. Still Life

William Harnett was a famous realist.

He went from Clonakilty to Philadelphia
in the aftermath of Famine. In

the same year the *London Illustrated News*
printed an etching of a woman.

On one arm was a baby—rigid, still.
In her other hand was a small dish.

They called it *Woman Begging at Clonakilty*.

I believe the surfaces of things
can barely hold in what is under them.

He became a painter.
He painted objects and instruments, household and musical.

He laid them on canvases with surfaces and textures
no light could exit from.

He painted his Cremona violin as if only he knew
the skin tones of spruce wood.

I drove through Clonakilty in early spring
when the air was tinged with a color close to vinegar,
a sure sign of rain,

past the corn store and the old linen mill,
down Long Quay.

I looked back at fields, at the air extracting
the essence of stillness from the afternoon.

(The child, of course, was dead.)

5. Silenced

In the ancient, gruesome story, Philomel
was little more than an ordinary girl.

She went away with her sister, Procne. Then
her sister's husband, Tereus, given to violence,
raped her once

and said he required her silence
forever. When she whispered *but*
he finished it all and had her tongue cut out.

Afterwards, she determined to tell her story
another way. She began a tapestry.
She gathered skeins, colors.
She started weaving.

She was weaving alone, in fact, and so intently
she never saw me enter.

An Irish sky was unfolding its wintry colors
slowly over my shoulder. An old radio
was there in the room as well, telling its own
unregarded story of violation.

Now she is rinsing the distances
with greenish silks. Now, for the terrible foreground,
she is pulling out crimson thread.

6. Histories

That was the year the news was always bad
(statistics on the radio)
the sad
truth no less so for being constantly repeated.

That was the year my mother was outside
in the shed
in her apron with the strings tied
twice behind her back and the door left wide.

7. Wisdom

The air hoarded frost. The lilac was a ghost
of lilac. It was eerie and expectant, both.
Metal touched clay, grated against stone. It was all
detailed, slow. Cigarettes were lit, there was laughter.
They were digging up an era, a city, my life.
They were using spades, machines, their wits.
I was standing there watching, on
a dry night in a small town in Ireland.
In this place, archaeology was not a science,
nor a search for the actual, nor a painstaking
catalog of parts and bone fragments, but
an art of memory and this, I thought, is how
legends have been, and will always be, edited—
not by saying them, but by unsettling
one layer of meaning from another and
another, and now they were pulling up something,
pushing its surface back into the world,
lifting it clear of its first funeral, moonlight
catching it, making it seem as if
it was swimming in and out of those gleams,
promising, disappearing. Then
I saw what it was—a plate, a round utensil,
a common flatness on which was served every day
the sustenance and restitution

of who we were once,
its substance braided with the dust of everything
that had happened since.
There was silence. No one looked up. Or spoke.
And then I knew I needed to tell you something:
The salmon of knowledge was fat and slick,
a sliver of freckles in the shallow water
and sought-after reflections of our old legends.
The hero ate the flesh and was wiser.
I wanted to say that to you. Then I woke.

8. Irish Interior

The woman sits and spins. She makes no sound.
The man behind her stands by the door.
There is always this: a background, a foreground.

This much we know. They do not want to be here.
The year is 1890. The inks have long since dried.
The name of the drawing is An Irish Interior.

The year is 1890. Before the inks are dry
Parnell will fall and orchards burn where the two
Captains—Moonlight, Boycott—have had their way.

She has a spinning wheel. He has a loom.
She has a shawl. He stands beside a landscape—
maybe a river, maybe hills, maybe even a farm

opening into a distance of water-song and a wood
they cannot reach: nothing belongs to them but this
melody and tyranny and hopelessness of thread

rendered by linework and the skewed perspective
the eye attains between his hand and the way
her hand rests on the wheel which goes to prove

only this: that there is always near and far, as
she works in one, he weaves inside the other.
Which we are in has yet to be made clear as

we stare through the lines until their lives
have almost disappeared and all we see, all
we want to see, are places in the picture light forgives,

such as the grain of the wood, the close seal of
the thread at the top of the loom and a door opening
into an afternoon they can never avail of.

9. In Our Own Country

They are making a new Ireland
at the end of our road,
under our very eyes,
under the arc lamps they aim and beam

into distances where we once lived,
into vistas we will never recognize.

We are here to watch.
We are looking for new knowledge.

They have been working here in all weathers
tearing away the road to our village—
bridge, path, river, all
lost under an onslaught of steel.

An old Europe
has come to us as a stranger in our city,
has forgotten its own music, wars and treaties,
is now a machine from the Netherlands or Belgium

dragging, tossing, breaking apart the clay
in which our timid spring used to arrive
with our daffodils in a single, crooked row.

Remember the emigrant boat?
Remember the lost faces burned in the last glances?
The air clearing away to nothing, nothing, nothing.

We pull our collars tightly round our necks
but the wind finds our throats,
predatory and wintry.

We walk home. What we know is this
(and this is all we know): we are now
and we will always be from now on—
for all I know we have always been—

exiles in our own country.

LETTERS TO THE DEAD

Amber

It never mattered that there was once a vast grieving:

trees on their hillsides, in their groves, weeping—
a plastic gold dropping

through seasons and centuries to the ground—
until now.

On this fine September afternoon from which you are absent
I am holding, as if my hand could store it,
an ornament of amber

you once gave me.

Reason says this:
The dead cannot see the living.
The living will never see the dead again.

The clear air we need to find each other in is
gone forever, yet

this resin once
collected seeds, leaves and even small feathers as it fell
and fell

which now in a sunny atmosphere seem as alive as
they ever were

as though the past could be present and memory itself
a Baltic honey—

a chafing at the edges of the seen, a showing off
    of just how much
can be kept safe

inside a flawed translucence.

An Elegy for My Mother in Which She Scarcely Appears

I knew we had to grieve for the animals
a long time ago: weep for them, pity them.
I knew it was our strange human duty
to write their elegies after we arranged their demise.
I was young then and able for the paradox.
I am older now and ready with the question:
what happened to them all? I mean to those
old dumb implements which have
no eyes to plead with us like theirs,
no claim to make on us like theirs? I mean—

there was a singing kettle. I want to know
why no one tagged its neck or ringed the tin
base of its extinct design or crouched to hear
its rising shriek in winter or wrote it down with
the birds in their blue sleeves of air
torn away with the trees that sheltered them.

And there were brass firedogs which lay out
all evening on the grate and in the heat
thrown at them by the last of the peat fire
but no one noted down their history or put them
in the old packs under slate-blue moonlight.
There was a wooden clotheshorse, absolutely steady

without sinews, with no mane and no meadows
to canter in; carrying, instead of
landlords or Irish monks, rinsed tea cloths
but still, I would have thought, worth adding to
the catalogue of what we need, what we always need

as is my mother, on this Dublin evening of
fog crystals and frost as she reaches out to test
one corner of a cloth for dryness as the prewar
Irish twilight closes in and down on the room
and the curtains are drawn and here am I,
not even born and already a conservationist,
with nothing to assist me but the last
and most fabulous of beasts—language, language—
which knows, as I do, that it's too late
to record the loss of these things but does so anyway,
and anxiously, in case it shares their fate.

And Soul

My mother died one summer—
the wettest in the records of the state.
Crops rotted in the west.
Checked tablecloths dissolved in back gardens.
Empty deck chairs collected rain.
As I took my way to her
through traffic, through lilacs dripping blackly
behind houses
and on curbsides, to pay her
the last tribute of a daughter, I thought of something
I remembered
I heard once, that the body is, or is
said to be, almost all
water and as I turned southward, that ours is
a city of it,
one in which
every single day the elements begin
a journey towards each other that will never,
given our weather,
fail—
          the ocean visible in the edges cut by it,
cloud color reaching into air,
the Liffey storing one and summoning the other,
salt greeting the lack of it at the North Wall and,

as if that wasn't enough, all of it
ending up almost every evening
inside our speech—
coast canal ocean river stream and now
mother and I drove on and although
the mind is unreliable in grief, at
the next cloudburst it almost seemed
they could be shades of each other,
the way the body is
of every one of them and now
they were on the move again—fog into mist,
mist into sea spray and both into the oily glaze
that lay on the railings of
the house she was dying in
as I went inside.

Secrets

Your coffin was so small.
Only I knew it was full of
candlewick bedspreads,
orange pekoe tea leaves
smoking chimneys over wet peat;

that steam rose there from
sweet winter herbs and pearl
onions and marrow bones
boiling all one afternoon
on the oven top in a stockpot,

and if I add the bolt of silk
you once brought home and
rolled out on a table, showing
the gloomy color pewter becomes
by candlelight, it is because

the secret histories of things
deserve to linger, to belong again
to the coil of your hair I found once
as a child, dried out by shadows,
in a shut-tight wooden box

in which was a mirror with
an ornate handle, an enameled back,
the original mercury amalgam
blemishing the glass from which
your face disappeared years ago.

On This Earth

We walk in sunshine to the Musée Marmottan. There,
on the wall opposite, I want to show you
Julie Manet

wearing her mother's brushstrokes,
clothed in the ochres of decorum, the hot bonnets
and silks of that century.

Hard to believe as we cross the road—the grass
dry, cropped and exhausted—that there was ever
a flood on this earth.

We leave the museum and go to a nearby café.
In the harsh noon light your cheeks are flushed.
The line is not perfect.

My first daughter you were my dove, my summer,
my skies lifting, my waters retreating,
my covenant with the earth.

Inheritance

I have been wondering
what I have to leave behind, to give my daughters.

No good offering the view
between here and Three Rock Mountain,
the blueness in the hours before rain, the long haze afterwards.
The ground I stood on was never really mine. It might not ever be theirs.

And gifts that were passed through generations—
silver and the fluid light left after silk—were never given here.

This is an island of waters, inland distances,
with a history of want and women who struggled
to make the nothing which was all they had
into something they could leave behind.

I learned so little from them: the lace bobbin with its braided mesh,
its oat-straw pillow and the wheat-colored shawl
knitted in one season
to imitate another

are all crafts I never had
and can never hand on. But then again there was a night
I stayed awake, alert and afraid, with my first child
who turned and turned; sick, fretful.

When dawn came I held my hand over the absence of fever,
over skin which had stopped burning, as if I knew the secrets
of health and air, as if I understood them

and listened to the silence
and thought, I must have learned that somewhere.

Traveler

The telescope was small, the moon high.
Whoever else was faint-hearted, she was not.
So, when the guests were gone, my mother started
her silvery and half-sized assault on
the New York skies.
A charcoal star: a showery, rosy fall
of sparks and her Sweet Afton cigarette
burning, circling in darkness as she steps back—
look at this she is calling out,
look and I do and I learn that this long
polished scrap of light is a traveler from
an age of ice and nothingness and has paused to hover
over the East River in the Cold War era.
November on the Hudson is windfall weather.
The East River is the earthly river.
There are other ones. They move inexorably,
back and forth, collecting and depositing
forever. I look again and what I see is not
helium nor energy nor an old outline of Long Island,
nor the elements that purify the space between
earth and atmosphere,
but the fishing port of Annagassan bay, its ruffled water,
the bend of the estuary,
the flat distances folding and unfolding, as far as
the eye can see, around its disappointed daughter.

Windfall

A small funeral finds its way in and out of shadow.

This late in the year, wildflowers are still there, still
dissolving the verge into a field—ragwort, knapweed,
samphire and rust harrow. There are windfalls underfoot.

This is the coffin of a young woman
who has left five children behind. There will be no obituary.
Words are required elsewhere:

We say *Mother Nature* when all we intend is
a woman was let die, out of sight, in a fever ward.

Look. In the distance you can see the estuary.
Feel under your feet October's rotten fruit.

Now say *Mother Ireland* when all that you mean is
there is no need to record this death in history.

Letters to the Dead

I

In the Old Kingdom scholars found pottery
written round and around with signs and marks.

II

Written in silt ware. On the rims of bowls.
Laid at the entrance to tombs.
Red with the iron of one world.
Set at the threshold of another.
They called them letters to the dead.

III

They did not mourn or grieve these signs or marks.
They were intimate, imploring, local, desperate.

IV

Here at the threshold of an Irish spring
you can no longer see
hawthorn bushes with their small ivory flowers
will soon come alive in every wind. Soon,
every hillside will be a distant bride.

V

If I could write it differently,
the secret history of a place,

as if it were a story of hidden water, known only
through the strange acoustic of a stream underfoot
in shallow grass,
it would be this—
this story.

VI

I wanted to bring you the gifts of the island,
the hawthorn in the last week of April,
the sight of the Liffey above Leixlip.
The willows there could be girls,
their hair still wet after a swim.
Instead, I have brought you a question.

VII

How many daughters stood alone at a grave,
and thought this of their mothers' lives?
That they were young in a country that hated a woman's body.
That they grew old in a country that hated a woman's body.

VIII

They asked for the counsel of the dead.
They asked for the power of the dead.
These are my letters to the dead.

INDOORS

To Memory

This is for you, goddess that you are.
This is a record for us both, this is a chronicle.
There should be more of them, they should be lyrical
and factual, and true, they should be written down
and spoken out on rainy afternoons, instead of which
they fall away; so I have written this, so it will not.
My last childless winter was the same
as all the other ones. Outside my window
the motherless landscape hoarded its own kind.
Light fattened the shadows; frost harried the snowdrops.
There was a logic to it, the way my mother loved astrology—
she came from a valley in the country
where everything that was haphazard and ill-timed
about our history had happened and so it seemed natural
that what she wanted most were the arts of the predetermined.
My child was born at the end of winter. How to prove it?
Not the child, of course, who slept in pre-spring darkness,
but the fact that the ocean—moonless, stripped of current—
entered the room quietly one evening and
lay down in the weave of the rug, and could be seen
shifting and sighing in blue-green sisal and I said
nothing about it, then or later, to anyone and when
the spring arrived I was ready to see a single field in
the distance on the Dublin hills allow its heathery color
to detach itself and come upstairs and settle in

the corner of the room farthest from the window.
I could, of course, continue. I could list for you
a whole inventory of elements and fixed entities
that broke away and found themselves disordered in
that season—assembling, dispersing—and without
a thought for laws that until then had barred
an apple flower from opening out at midnight
or lilac rooting in the coldest part of ocean. Then
it stopped. Little by little what was there came back.
Slowly at first; then surely. I realized what had happened
was secret, hardly possible, to be remembered always,
which is why you are listening as rain comes down,
restored to its logic, responsive to air and land
and I am telling you this: you are after all
not simply the goddess of memory, you have
nine daughters yourself and can understand.

Of Shadow. Of Simile

One afternoon of summer rain
my hand skimmed a shelf and I found
an old florin. Ireland, 1950.

We say *like* or *as* and the world is
a fish minted in silver and alloy,

an outing for all the children,
an evening in the Sandford cinema,
a paper cone of lemonade crystals and

say it again so we can see
androgyny of angels, edges to a circle,
the way the body works against the possible—

and no one to tell us, now or ever,
why it ends, why
it has to end:

I am holding
two whole shillings of nothing,
observing its heaviness, its uselessness.

And how in the cool shadow of nowhere
a salmon leaps up to find a weir
it could not even know
was never there.

Indoors

I have always wanted a world that is cured of the outdoors.
A household without gods.
Walls arriving, entrances taking shape, verticals meeting
horizontals: a *where* fetching a *now*.

Find me a word for love. Make it *damp*. Sinuous companion,
knowing how to enter, settle in wood, salt the sheets
with cold, saying by this that we could never be
anything but an island people.

There is always a place where a fable starts—where a god
proves he is a god by adding
not simply wings and sinews to his shoulders

but the horizon swinging up—rivers, mountains, headlights
only slowly
righting themselves as he rises to find
the first signs of day becoming night.

So it was above our neighborhood, the world straightening
under wings, the noise of discord
clearly audible, the hinterland reaching to the sea,
its skin a map of wounds, its history a treatise of infections.

But I was an indoor nature poet,
safe in my countryside
of handles and entrances, my pastoral of inland elements,

holding against my face the lured-in aftermath
of ocean, atmosphere: the intimate biography of damp
in the not-dry feel of a child's cardigan.

In Season

The man and woman on the blue and white
mug we have owned for so long
we can hardly remember
where we got it
or how

are not young. They are out walking in
a cobalt dusk under the odd azure of
apple blossom,
going towards each other with hands outstretched.

Suddenly this evening, for the first time,
I wondered *how will they find each other?*

For so long
they have been circling the small circumference
of an ironstone cup that they have forgotten,
if they ever really knew it, earth itself.

This top to bottom endlessly turning world
in which they only meet
each other meeting
each other
has no seasons, no intermission; and if

they do not know when light is rearranged
according to the usual celestial ordinance—
tides, stars, a less and later dusk—
and if they never noticed

the cotton edge of the curtains brightening earlier
on a spring morning after the clocks have changed
and changed again, it can only be

they have their own reasons, since
they have their own weather (a sudden fog,
tinted rain) which they have settled into

so that the kettle steam, the splash of new tea are
a sought-after climate endlessly folded
into a rinsed horizon.

The Room in Which My First Child Slept

After a while I thought of it this way:
It was a town underneath a mountain
crowned by snow and every year a river
rushed through, enveloping the dusk
in a noise everyone knew signaled spring—
a small town, known for a kind of calico,
made there, strong and unglazed,
a makeshift of cotton in which the actual
unseparated husks still remained and
could be found if you looked behind
the coarse daisies and the red-billed bird
with swept-back wings always trying to
arrive safely on the inch or so of cotton it
might have occupied if anyone had offered it.
And if you ask me now what happened to it—
the town that is—the answer is, of course,
there was no town, it never actually
existed, and the calico, the glazed cotton
on which a bird never landed is not gone,
because it never was, never once, but then
how to explain that sometimes I can hear
the river in those first days of April, making
its way through the dusk, having learned
to speak the way I once spoke, saying
as if I didn't love you
as if I wouldn't have died for you.

Midnight on the Sixth Day

On the Chi-Rho page of the Book of Kells
X, P and I are intertwined. They are the initials of Christ.

    The letters are picked out in drops of lead. They are Coptic,
    Pictic, Greek in origin.

I am reading from a book of Irish manuscripts. It is late
and I have laid it on the table.

    Out at the back door our cat is waiting.
    When she comes in her eyes are dark sugar.

What's stuck in her coat is all the ways that summer
can stripe itself.

    Surely he must have known, the old master,
    that he was making shock waves for the sacred?

(In the corner of his page below the initials
an otter is eating a fish, a mouse is nibbling at the Eucharist.)

Neighbors

The skies above Dundrum tonight, unusually,
are clear of rain and wide.

This is the hour of gathering.

We call the children in.
We stow the bikes and close the garage doors.

The worker-stars are up. They lift and carry—

a child, a sheaf of wheat, a whole horizon.

They have till dawn to set
the ships on course, the compasses dead straight.

When we look up the distances are lost on us.

Everything seems near and purposeful.

And bright. And side by side.

Falling Asleep to the Sound of Rain

Understanding where you live is first of all
knowing its noises which are memorized
without you knowing that they are, for instance

weather: starting after midnight after stillness
is the *clink-clink* Irish rain makes on its journey in
a garden in the suburbs, falling on out of season

jasmine then iron railings between
my neighbor's house and mine; which began at sea.

I loved small towns—they seemed to come from
a kinder time: shop blinds lowered on weekday
afternoons, peaceful evenings with beds turned down,

shoes gathering, two by two, under them and in
the cellars of nearby farms, stopped up, ready
to be sold on market day, oily, sharp cheddars,

getting sharper, growing older. But the truth is
there is no truth in this. I never lived there.

What would it mean, I used to wonder, to leave
everything you knew, leave it altogether, never mention
memories; start again inside that reticence?

I once drove into Tarbert at dawn. Everything was gone.
No distances; no trees. Only imagined ones.
I had to begin making my own pageant of

small hawthorn flowers, elderberry. We love fog because
it shifts old anomalies into the elements
surrounding them. It gives relief from a way of seeing.

It is the gift of sleep or the approach to sleep,
to make component parts of place and consciousness
meaningless and, as breathing slows down,

to do what water does, announce a source in cadence,
repetition, sound, allow a gradual dissolving of
boundaries between the actual and evident and still,

when all that is done, I know there never was
a single place for me. I never lost enough to have one.

I want to live where they refused to speak—
those first emigrants who never said
where they came from, what they left behind.

Their country was a finger to the lips, a child's question stopped.
And yet behind their eyes in eerie silence, was an island,
if you looked for it: bronze-green perch in a mute river.

Peat smoke rising from soundless kindling.
Rain falling on leaves and iron, making no noise at all.

BECOMING THE HAND OF JOHN SPEED

Atlantis — A Lost Sonnet

How on earth did it happen, I used to wonder
that a whole city—arches, pillars, colonnades,
not to mention vehicles and animals—had all
one fine day gone under?

I mean, I said to myself, the world was small then.
Surely a great city must have been missed?
I miss our old city—

white pepper, white pudding, you and I meeting
under fanlights and low skies to go home in it. Maybe
what really happened is

this: the old fable-makers searched hard for a word
to convey that what is gone is gone forever and
never found it. And so, in the best traditions of

where we come from, they gave their sorrow a name
and drowned it.

Becoming the Hand of John Speed

How do you make a nation?
How do you make it answer to you?
How do you make its parts, its waterways
its wished-for blueness at the horizon point
take heed?

I have no answer. I was born in a nation
I had no part in making.

But sometimes late at night when I want to imagine
what it was to be a part of it
I take down my book and then I am

the agile mapping hand of John Speed
making *The Kingdome of Ireland, 1612,*

my pen moving over a swerve of contour,
my ink stroke adding an acre of ocean.

The Dublin hills surrender two dimensions.
Forests collapse, flattening all their wolves.

The Irish sea
cedes its ancient tensions,
its gannets, gulls, cormorants all stopped
from flying away by their own silhouettes—

and you might say my nation has become
all but unrecognizable, but no,

I remember the way it was when I was young,
wanting the place to know me at first glance
and it never did,
it never did, and so

this is the way to have it, cut to size,
its waters burned in copper, its air unbreathed
its future neighborhoods almost all unnamed—

and even the old, ocean-shaped horizon
surprised by its misshapen accuracy—

ready and flat and yearning to be claimed.

Papers

I hold my father's passport.
I hold a spring dawn, clearing eastwards.

I hold the night train on its way from Paris to Berlin.

These are the nineteen thirties.
This is a new nation
he has a hand in making. Say that the ages

have opened, that history has relented,
that a new Ireland—

all sovereign rhetoric and self-doubt and shortages—
is folded inside the milled
cardboard of these pages as

mysterious villages grow plainer,
starlight leaves behind charcoal-colored fields

and from his train window he is looking out at
the *here now then*

of places whose histories will continue
long after their borders have ceased to—

which is how I see him
which is where I leave him
as I hand his papers to a pair of uniformed officers

who stare incuriously at this record of departures from
a country whose name, given all the circumstances,
they may never need to get used to.

Formation

1.

The boredom of the spring afternoon.
The aftermath of rain. The ground soggy with it.

Geography class in the upstairs room, facing the bay.

Eavan, do you know how an island is formed?

Pronunciation: 'I-lənd
Function: noun
Etymology: alteration (influenced by Anglo-French isle) of
earlier iland, from Middle English, from Old English īgland
(akin to Old Norse eyland), from īg island (akin to Old English
ēa river, Latin aqua water) + land land
1 : a tract of land surrounded by water and smaller than a continent

2.

Midnight—a sound of car alarms and sirens.

I am reading a novel of nineteenth-century Ireland.

Sedition is in the air. Betrayal is in the future.

My face is caught
in the coarse waters of polished lemon wood.

What is the body anyway but a stranger
bringing news of somewhere else?

In the distance I can hear the Kish lighthouse—
a phrase from the coast, saying salt water, saying danger.

On Seeing James Malton's Powerscourt-House, Dublin 1795

Closed as I was
day after day
into that city, with
its iron, ocean, air,
composed of a single, perfect,
shade of gray
I never believed there were others,
their eyes half-shut,
a harsh, determined line to their mouth,
and their hats with falling brims
in the direct light
of the far south
writing down names and names:

the secrets of the lily,
the life of the amaryllis,
a single eyelid scarred
with a million years opening,
closing, opening on
the one dying lizard—
(naming the earth
seemed to me then
only a gateway to death.)

The beautiful city died,
was made extinct,
a city with huge wings,
a city with rare habits,
what good did it do to name it?

I let the question rise and grow into rays
of weak Irish sunlight,
the start of another day
on a paved Dublin street
and praise the engraver's art—
the gloomy studio,
aquatinta, *mezzotinto*, dry point, steel point,
the wax where it lies
on a copper surface, the burnisher beside it—

the acid-smelling rooms
where nothing ever dies.

The Nineteenth-Century Irish Poets

Once I thought about them in a different way. I thought

they came from a small island. They stayed in one place.
They lived their lives. Kept their counsel. Held their peace.

But now, looking back, I think they were poisoned—
every word they used contaminated by the one it was not.

Now, when I take the book down after midnight,
I read every line as if it came from a burned throat.

Now I see what it is they left us. The toxic lyric.

The poem for which there is no antidote.

The Origins of Our Native Speech

Ours was a nation of fever, or so
we heard when we were young,
contagion waiting for us
at every turn, in

the dwindling marsh saxifrage,
the sedge by the lake, even
cow parsley, even
bog cottons, and

if our elders couldn't find it there
they burned and burned—
smoke rising from
back gardens

and rising with the odor of
old bedding—everything
thrown on those
cleansing flames.

There was a lore to it. That it knew
how to hide, how to wait, so
we too became
in time, children

of fear, looking to find it as they did,
leaning down over stagnant
waters at dawn,
sensing dry

heat, a thirst nothing could slake,
the words we spoke
coming back to us
fractured by delirium.

Violence Against Women

Once in the West Pennines I was shown
the source of the Industrial Revolution—
the first streams harnessed to the wheels
which drove the mills which spun out textiles
which emptied out the cottages and hillsides
and sent men and women down to Hades.
(Fast water and mountains without lime
and greed all complicit in the shame.)

Real men and women, flesh and blood
and long dead and ready to be understood—
and not those abandoned and unsaved
women who died here who never lived:

mindless, sexless, birthless, only sunned
by shadows, only dressed in muslin,
shepherdesses of the English pastoral
waiting for the return of an English April
that never came and never will again.

Wheels turned, the jenny worked, a plain-
spoken poetry was chanted by the flow
and finished them. They were the last to know
what happened in this north-facing twilight,

the aftermath I saw here, staring at
an old site of injury, a hurt
that never healed and never can. O art,

O empire and the arranged relations,
so often covert, between power and cadence,
tell me what it is you have done with
the satin bonnets and the pastel sun, with
the women gathering their unreal sheep
into real verse for whom no one will weep?

Instructions

To write about age you need to take something and break it.

(This is an art that has always loved young women. And silent ones.)

A branch, perhaps, girlish with blossom. Snapped off. Close to the sap.

Then cut through a promised summer. Continue. Cut down to the root.

The spring afternoon will come to your door, angry as any mother. Ignore her.

Now take syntax. Break that too. What is left is for you and you only:

A dead tree. The future. What does not bear fruit. Or thinking of.

In Coming Days

Soon
I will be as old as the Shan Van Vocht—

(although no one knows how old she is).

Soon
I will ask to meet her on the borders of Kildare.

It will be cold.
The hazel willow will be frozen by the wayside.

The rag-taggle of our history
will march by us.

They will hardly notice two women by the roadside.

I will speak to her. Even though I know
she can only speak with words made by others.

I will say to her. You were betrayed.
Do you know that?

She will look past me at the torn banners,
makeshift pikes, bruised feet. Her lips will move:

To the Currach of Kildare
The boys they will repair.

There is still time, I will tell her. We can still
grow older together.

And will Ireland then be free?
And will Ireland then be free?

We loved the same things, I will say—
or at least some of them. Once in fact, long ago,

Yes! Ireland shall be free,
From the center to the sea.

I almost loved you.